THE LOST LEMURIA

With Two Maps Showing
Distribution of Land Areas at Different Periods

SALMON BOOKS

THE LOST LEMURIA

With Two Maps Showing

Distribution of Land Areas at Different Periods

W. Scott-Elliot

Author of "The Story of Atlantis,"

"Man's Places in the Universe," etc.

SALMON BOOKS

Chennai New Delhi

SALMON BOOKS

ISBN 9789349032361

Salmon Books
No. 44, Nallathambi Street,
Triplicane, Chennai 600 005

Printed and bound in India

MJP 077

Publisher: **C. Janarthanan**

PUBLISHER'S NOTE

The legacy of a country is in its varied cultural heritage, historical literature, developments in the field of economy and science. The top nations in the world are competing in the field of science, economy and literature. This vast legacy has to be conserved and documented so that it can be bestowed to the future generation. The knowledge of this legacy is slowly getting perished in the present generation due to lack of documentation.

Keeping this in mind, the concern with retrospective acquiring of rare books has been accented recently by the bur-geoning reprint industry. Salmon Books is gratified to retrieve the rare collections with a view to bring back those books that were landmarks in their time.

In this effort, a series of rare books would be republished under the banner, "Salmon Books". The books in the reprint series have been carefully selected for their contemporary usefulness as well as their historical importance within the intellectual. We reconstruct the book with slight enhance-ments made for better presentation, without affecting the contents of the original edition.

Most of the works selected for republishing covers a huge range of subjects, from history to anthropology. We believe this reprint edition will be a service to the numerous researchers and practitioners active in this fascinating field. We allow readers to experience the wonder of peering into a scholarly work of the highest order and seminal significance.

Salmon Books

The object of this paper is not so much to bring forward new and startling information about the lost continent of Lemuria and its inhabitants, as to establish by the evidence obtainable from geology and from the study of the relative distribution of living and extinct animals and plants, as well as from the observed processes of physical evolution in the lower kingdoms, the facts stated in the "Secret Doctrine" and in other works with reference to these now submerged lands.

The Lost Lemuria.

It is generally recognised by science that what is now dry land, on the surface of our globe, was once the ocean floor, and that what is now the ocean floor was once dry land. Geologists have in some cases been able to specify the exact portions of the earth's surface where these subsidences and upheavals have taken place, and although the lost continent of Atlantis has so far received scant recognition from the world of science, the general concensus of opinion has for long pointed to the existence, at some pre-historic time, of a vast southern continent to which the name of Lemuria has been assigned.

Evidence supplied by Geology and by the relative distribution of living and extinct Animals and Plants.

"The history of the earth's development shows us that the distribution of land and water on its surface is ever and continually changing. In consequence of geological changes of the earth's crust, *elevations* and *depressions* of the ground take place everywhere, sometimes more strongly marked in one place, sometimes in another. Even if they happen so slowly that in the course of centuries the seashore rises or sinks only a few inches, or even only a few lines, still they nevertheless effect great results in the course of long periods of time. And long—immeasurably long—periods of time have not been wanting in the earth's history. During the course of many millions of years, ever since organic life existed on the earth, land and water have perpetually struggled for supremacy. Continents and islands have sunk into the sea, and new ones have arisen out of its bosom. Lakes and seas have been slowly raised and dried up, and new water basins have arisen by the sinking of the ground. Peninsulas have become islands by the narrow neck of land which connected them with the mainland sinking into the water. The islands of an archipelago have become the peaks of a continuous chain of mountains by the whole floor of their sea being considerably raised.

"Thus the Mediterranean at one time was an inland sea, when in the place of the Straits of Gibraltar, an isthmus connected Africa with Spain. England even during the more recent history of the earth, when man already existed, has repeatedly been connected with the European continent and been repeatedly separated from it. Nay, even Europe and North America have been directly connected. The South Sea at one time formed a large Pacific Continent, and the numerous little islands which now lie scattered in it were simply the highest peaks of the mountains covering that continent. The Indian Ocean formed a continent which extended from the Sunda Islands along the southern coast of Asia to the east coast of Africa. This large continent of former times Sclater, an Englishman, has called *Lemuria*, from the monkey-like animals which inhabited it, and it is at the same time of great importance from being the probable cradle of the human race, which in all likelihood here first developed out of anthropoid apes.* The important proof which Alfred Wallace has furnished, by the help of chorological facts, that the present Malayan Archipelago consists in reality of two completely different divisions, is particularly interesting. The western division, the Indo-Malayan Archipelago, comprising the large islands of

* Haeckel is correct enough in his surmise that Lemuria was the cradle of the human race as it now exists, but it was not out of Anthropoid apes that mankind developed. A reference will be made later on to the position in nature which the Anthropoid apes really occupy.

Borneo, Java and Sumatra, was formerly connected by Malacca with the Asiatic continent, and probably also with the Lemurian continent just mentioned. The eastern division on the other hand, the Austro-Malayan Archipelago, comprising Celebes, the Moluccas, New Guinea, Solomon's Islands, etc., was formerly directly connected with Australia. Both divisions were formerly two continents separated by a strait, but they have now for the most part sunk below the level of the sea. Wallace, solely on the ground of his accurate chorological observations, has been able in the most accurate manner to determine the position of this former strait, the south end of which passes between Balij and Lombok.

"Thus, ever since liquid water existed on the earth, the boundaries of water and land have eternally changed, and we may assert that the outlines of continents and islands have never remained for an hour, nay, even for a minute, exactly the same. For the waves eternally and perpetually break on the edge of the coast, and whatever the land in these places loses in extent, it gains in other places by the accumulation of mud, which condenses into solid stone and again rises above the level of the sea as new land. Nothing can be more erroneous than the idea of a firm and unchangeable outline of our continents, such as is impressed upon us in early youth by defective lessons on geography, which are devoid of a geological basis."*

The name Lemuria, as above stated, was originally adopted by Mr. Sclater in recognition of the fact that it was propably on this continent that animals of the Lemuroid type were developed.

"This," writes A. R. Wallace, "is undoubtedly a legitimate and highly probable supposition, and it is an example of the way in which a study of the geographical distribution of animals may enable us to reconstruct the geography of a bygone age.

* Ernst Haeckel's "Hist. of Creation," 2nd ed., 1876, Vol. 1., pp. 360-62.

It [this continent] represents what was probably a primary zoological region in some past geological epoch; but what that epoch was and what were the limits of the region in question, we are quite unable to say. If we are to suppose that it comprised the whole area now inhabited by Lemuroid animals, we must make it extend from West Africa to Burmah, South China and Celebes, an area which it possibly did once occupy."*

"We have already had occasion," he elsewhere writes, "to refer to an ancient connection between this sub-region (the Ethiopian) and Madagascar, in order to explain the distribution of the Lemurine type, and some other curious affinities between the two countries. This view is supported by the geology of India, which shows us Ceylon and South India consisting mainly of granite and old-metamorphic rocks, while the greater part of the peninsula is of tertiary formation, with a few isolated patches of secondary rocks. It is evident, therefore, that during much of the tertiary period,† Ceylon and South India were bounded on the north by a considerable extent of sea, and probably formed part of an extensive Southern Continent or great island. The very numerous and remarkable cases of affinity with Malaya, require, however, some closer approximation with these islands, which probably occurred at a later period. When, still later, the great plains and tablelands of Hindostan were formed, and a permanent land communication effected with the rich and highly developed Himalo-Chinese fauna, a rapid immigration of new types took place, and many of the less

* Alfred Russell Wallace's "The Geographical Distribution of Animals—with a study of the relations of living and extinct Faunas as elucidating the past changes of the Earth's Surface." London: Macmillan & Co., 1876. Vol. I., pp. 76-7.

† Ceylon and South India, it is true, have been bounded on the north by a considerable extent of sea, but that was at a much earlier date than the Tertiary period.

specialised forms of mammalia and birds became extinct. Among reptiles and insects the competition was less severe, or the older forms were too well adapted to local conditions to be expelled; so that it is among these groups alone that we find any considerable number of what are probably the remains of the ancient fauna of a now submerged Southern Continent."*

After stating that during the whole of the tertiary and perhaps during much of the secondary periods, the great land masses of the earth were probably situated in the Northern Hemisphere, Wallace proceeds, "In the Southern Hemisphere there appear to have been three considerable and very ancient land masses, varying in extent from time to time, but always keeping distinct from each other, and represented more or less completely by Australia, South Africa and South America of our time. Into these flowed successive waves of life as they each in turn became temporarily united with some part of the Northern land."†

Although, apparently in vindication of some conclusions of his which had been criticised by Dr. Hartlaub, Wallace subsequently denied the necessity of postulating the existence of such a continent, his general recognition of the facts of subsidences and upheavals of great portions of the earth's surface, as well as the inferences which he draws from the acknowledged relations of living and extinct faunas as above stated, remain of course unaltered.

The following extracts from Mr. H. F. Blandford's most interesting paper read before a meeting of the Geological Society deals with the subject in still greater detail‡:—

* Wallace's "Geographical Distribution, etc." Vol. 1, pp. 328-9.

† Wallace's "Geographical Distribution, etc.," Vol. ii., p. 155.

‡ H. F. Blandford "On the age and correlations of the Plant-bearing series of India and the former existence of an Indo-Oceanic Continent," see Quarterly Journal of the Geological Society, Vol. xxxi., 1875, pp. 534-540.

"The affinities between the fossils of both animals and plants of the Beaufort group of Africa and those of the Indian Panchets and Kathmis are such as to suggest the former existence of a land connexion between the two areas. But the resemblance of the African and Indian fossil faunas does not cease with Permian and Triassic times. The plant beds of the Uitenhage group have furnished eleven forms of plants, two of which Mr. Tate has identified with Indian Rájmahál plants. The Indian Jurassic fossils have yet to be described (with a few exceptions), but it has been stated that Dr. Stoliezka was much struck with the affinities of certain of the Cutch fossils to African forms; and Dr. Stoliezka and Mr. Griesbach have shown that of the Cretaceous fossils of the Umtafuni river in Natal, the majority (22 out of 35 described forms) are identical with species from Southern India. Now the plant-bearing series of India and the Karoo and part of the Uitenhage formation of Africa are in all probability of fresh-water origin, both indicating the existence of a large land area around, from the waste of which these deposits are derived. Was this land continuous between the two regions? And is there anything in the present physical geography of the Indian Ocean which would suggest its probable position? Further, what was the connexion between this land and Australia which we must equally assume to have existed in Permian times? And, lastly, are there any peculiarities in the existing fauna and flora of India, Africa and the intervening islands which would lend support to the idea of a former connexion more direct than that which now exists between Africa and South India and the Malay peninsula? The speculation here put forward is no new one. It has long been a subject of thought in the minds of some Indian and European naturalists, among the former of whom I may mention my brother [Mr. Blandford] and Dr. Stoliezka, their speculations being grounded on the relationship and partial identity of the faunas and floras of past times, not less than on that existing community of forms which has led Mr. Andrew Murray, Mr. Searles, V. Wood, jun., and Professor Huxley to infer the existence of a Miocene continent occupying a part of the Indian Ocean. Indeed, all that I can pretend to aim at in this paper is to endeavour to give some additional definition and extension to the conception of its geological aspect.

" With regard to the geographical evidence, a glance at the map will show that from the neighbourhood of the West Coast of India to that of the Seychelles, Madagascar, and the Mauritius, extends a line af coral atolls and banks, including Adas bank, the Laccadives, Maldives, the Chagos group and the Saya de Mulha, all indicating the existence of a submerged mountain range or ranges. The Seychelles, too, are mentioned by Mr. Darwin as rising from an extensive and tolerably level bank having a depth of between 30 and 40 fathoms ; so that, although now partly encircled by fringing reefs, they may be regarded as a virtual extension of the same submerged axis. Further west the Cosmoledo and Comoro Islands consist of atolls and islands surrounded by barrier reefs ; and these bring us pretty close to the present shores of Africa and Madagascar. It seems at least probable that in this chain of atolls, banks, and barrier reefs we have indicated the position of an ancient mountain chain, which possibly formed the back-bone of a tract of later Palæozoic Mesozoic, and early Tertiary land, being related to it much as the Alpine and Himálayan system is to the Europæo - Asiatic continent, and the Rocky Mountains and Andes to the two Americas. As it is desirable to designate this Mesozoic land by a name, I would propose that of Indo-Oceana. [The name given to it by Mr. Sclater, *viz.*, Lemuria, is, however, the one which has been most generally adopted.] Professor Huxley has suggested on palæontological grounds that a land connexion existed in this region (or rather between Abyssinia and India) during the Miocene epoch. From what has been said above it will be seen that I infer its existence from a far earlier date.* With regard to its depression, the only present evidence relates to its northern extremity, and shows that it was in this region, later than the great trap-flows of the Dakhan. These enormous sheets of volcanic rock are remarkably horizontal to the east of the Gháts and the Sakyádri range, but to the west of this they begin to dip seawards, so that the island of Bombay is composed of the higher parts of the formation. This indicates only that the depression to the westward has taken place in Tertiary times; and to that extent Professor Huxley's inference, that it was after the Miocene period, is quite consistent with the geological evidence."

After proceeding at some length to instance the close relationship of many of the fauna in the lands under consideration (Lion, Hyæna, Jackal, Leopard, Antelope, Gazelle, Sand-grouse, Indian Bustard, many Land Molusca, and notably the Lemur and the Scaly Anteater) the writer proceeds as follows:—

"Palæontology, physical geography and geology, equally with the ascertained distribution of living animals and plants, offer thus their concurrent testimony to the former close connexion of Africa and India, including the tropical islands of the Indian Ocean. This Indo-Oceanic land appears to have existed from at least early Permian times, probably (as Professor Huxley has pointed out) up to the close of the Miocene epoch;† and South Africa and Peninsular India are the existing remnants of that ancient land. It may not have been absolutely continuous during the whole of this long period. Indeed, the Cretaceous

* A reference to the maps will show that Mr. Blandford's estimate of date is the more correct of the two.

† Parts of the continent of course endured, but the dismemberment of Lemuria is said to have taken place before the beginning of the Eocene Age.

rocks of Southern India and Southern Africa, and the marine Jurassic beds of the same regions, prove that some portions of it were, for longer or shorter periods, invaded by the sea; but any break of continuity was probably not prolonged; for Mr. Wallace's investigations in the Eastern Archipelago have shown how narrow a sea may offer an insuperable barrier to the migration of land animals. In Palæozoic times this land must have been connected with Australia, and in Tertiary times with Malayana, since the Malayan forms with African alliances are in several cases distinct from those of India. We know as yet too little of the geology of the eastern peninsula to say from what epoch dates its connexion with Indo-Oceanic land. Mr. Theobald has ascertained the existence of Triassic, Cretaceous, and Nummulitic rocks in the Arabian coast range; and Carboniferous limestone is known to occur from Moulmein southward, while the range east of the Irrawadi is formed of younger Tertiary rocks. From this it would appear that a considerable part of the Malay peninsula must have been occupied by the sea during the greater part of the Mesozoic and Eocene periods. Plant-bearing rocks of Ráníganj age have been identified as forming the outer spurs of the Sikkim Himálaya; the ancient land must therefore have extended some distance to the north of the present Gangetic delta. Coal both of Cretaceous and Tertiary age occurs in the Khasi hills, and also in Upper Assam, but in both cases associated with marine beds; so that it would appear that in this region the boundaries of land and sea oscillated somewhat during Cretaceous and Eocene times. To the north-west of India the existence of great formations of Cretaceous and Nummulitic age, stretching far through Baluchistán and Persia, and entering into the structure of the north-west Himálaya, prove that in the later Mesozoic and Eocene ages India had no direct communication with western Asia; while the Jurassic rocks of Cutch, the Salt range, and the northern Himálaya, show that in the preceding period the sea covered a large part of the present Indus basin; and the Triassic, Carboniferous, and still more recent marine formations of the Himálaya, indicate that from very early times till the upheaval of that great chain, much of its present site was for ages covered by the sea.

" To sum up the views advanced in this paper.

" 1st. The plant-bearing series of India ranges from early Permian to the latest Jurassic times, indicating (except in a few cases and locally) the uninterrupted continuity of land and fresh water conditions. These may have prevailed from much earlier times.

" 2nd. In the early Permian, as in the Postpliocene age, a cold climate prevailed down to low latitudes, and I am inclined to believe in both hemispheres simultaneously. With the decrease of cold the flora and reptilian fauna of Permian times were diffused to Africa, India, and possibly Australia; or the flora may have existed in Australia somewhat earlier, and have been diffused thence.

" 3rd. India, South Africa and Australia were connected by an Indo-Oceanic Continent in the Permian epoch; and the two former countries remained connected (with at the utmost only short interruptions) up to the end of the Miocene period. During the latter part of the time this land was also connected with Malayana.

" 4th. In common with some previous writers, I consider that the position of this land was defined by the range of coral reefs and banks that now exist between the Arabian sea and East Africa.

" 5th. Up to the end of the Nummulitic epoch no direct connexion (except possibly for short periods) existed between India and Western Asia."

In the discussion which followed the reading of the paper, Professor Ramsay "agreed with the author in the belief in the junction of Africa with India and Australia in geological times."

Mr. Woodward "was pleased to find that the author had added further evidence, derived from the fossil flora of the mesozoic series of India, in corroboration of the views of Huxley, Sclater and others as to the former existence of an old submerged continent ('Lemuria') which Darwin's researches on coral reefs had long since foreshadowed."

"Of the five now existing continents," writes Ernst Haeckel, in his great work "The History of Creation,"* "neither Australia, nor America, nor Europe can have been this primæval home [of man], or the so-called 'Paradise,' the 'cradle of the human race.' Most circumstances indicate Southern Asia as the locality in question. Besides Southern Asia, the only other of the now existing continents which might be viewed in this light is Africa. But there are a number of circumstances (especially chorological facts) which suggest that the primeval home of man was a continent now sunk below the surface of the Indian Ocean, which extended along the south of Asia, as it is at present (and probably in direct connection with it), towards the east, as far as Further India and the Sunda Islands; towards the west, as far as Madagascar and the south-eastern shores of Africa. We have already mentioned that many facts in animal and vegetable geography render the former existence of such a South Indian continent very probable. Sclater has given this continent the name of Lemuria, from the semi-apes which were characteristic of it. By assuming this Lemuria to have been man's primæval home, we greatly facilitate the explanation of the geographical distribution of the human species by migration."

In a subsequent work, "The Pedigree of Man," Haeckel asserts

* Vol ii., pp. 325-6.

the existence of Lemuria at some early epoch of the earth's history as an acknowledged fact.

The following quotation from Dr. Hartlaub's writings may bring to a close this portion of the evidence in favour of the existence of the lost Lemuria* :—

"Five and thirty years ago, Isidore Geoffroy St. Hilaire remarked that, if one had to classify the Island of Madagascar exclusively on zoological considerations, and without reference to its geographical situation, it could be shown to be neither Asiatic nor African, but quite different from either, and almost a fourth continent. And this fourth continent could be further proved to be, as regards its fauna, much more different from Africa, which lies so near to it, than from India which is so far away. With these words the correctness and pregnancy of which later investigations tend to bring into their full light, the French naturalist first stated the interesting problem for the solution of which an hypothesis based on scientific knowledge has recently been propounded, for this fourth continent of Isidore Geoffroy is Sclater's 'Lemuria'—that sunken land which, containing parts of Africa, must have extended far eastwards over Southern India and Ceylon, and the highest points of which we recognise in the volcanic peaks of Bourbon and Mauritius, and in the central range of Madagascar itself—the last resorts of the almost extinct Lemurine race which formerly peopled it."

Evidence obtained from Archaic Records.

The further evidence we have with regard to Lemuria and its inhabitants has been obtained from the same source and in the same manner as that which resulted in the writing of the *Story of Atlantis*. In this case also the author has been privileged to obtain copies of two maps, one representing Lemuria

* Dr. G. Hartlaub "On the Avifauna of Madagascar and the Mascarene Islands," see "The Ibis," a Quarterly Journal of Ornithology. Fourth Series, Vol. i., 1877, p. 334.

(and the adjoining lands) during the period of that continent's greatest expansion, the other exhibiting its outlines after its dismemberment by great catastrophes, but long before its final destruction.

It was never professed that the maps of Atlantis were correct *to a single degree* of latitude, or longitude, but, with the far greater difficulty of obtaining the information in the present case, it must be stated that still less must these maps of Lemuria be taken as absolutely accurate. In the former case there was a globe, a good bas-relief in terra-cotta, and a well-preserved map on parchment, or skin of some sort, to copy from. In the present case there was only a broken terra-cotta model and a very badly preserved and crumpled map, so that the difficulty of carrying back the remembrance of all the details, and consequently of reproducing exact copies, has been far greater.

We were told that it was by mighty Adepts in the days of Atlantis that the Atlantean maps were produced, but we are not aware whether the Lemurian maps were fashioned by some of the divine instructors in the days when Lemuria still existed, or in still later days of the Atlantean epoch.

But while guarding against over-confidence in the absolute accuracy of the maps in question, the transcriber of the archaic originals believes that they may in all important particulars, be taken as approximately correct.

Probable Duration of the Continent of Lemuria.

A period—speaking roughly—of between four and five million years probably represents the life of the continent of Atlantis, for it is about that time since the Rmoahals, the first sub-race of the Fourth Root Race who inhabited Atlantis, arose on a portion of the Lemurian Continent which at that time still existed. Remembering that in the evolutionary process the figure four invariably represents not only the nadir of the cycle, but the period of shortest duration, whether in the case of a Manvantara or of a race, it may be assumed that the number of millions of years assignable as the life-limit of the continent of Lemuria must be very much greater than that representing the life of Atlantis, the continent of the Fourth Root Race. But in the case of Lemuria no dates can be stated with even approximate accuracy. Geological epochs, so far as they are known to modern science, will be a better medium for contemporary reference, and they alone will be dealt with.

The Maps. But not even geological epochs, it will be observed, are assigned to the maps. If, however, an inference may be drawn from all the evidence before us, it would seem probable that the older of the two Lemurian maps represented the earth's configuration from the Permian, through the Triassic and into the Jurassic epoch, while the second map probably represents the earth's configuration through the Cretaceous and into the Eocene period.

From the older of the two maps it may be seen that the equatorial continent of Lemuria at the time of its greatest expansion nearly girdled the globe, extending as it then did from the site of the present Cape Verd Islands a few miles from the coast of Sierra Leone, in a south-easterly direction through Africa, Australia, the Society Islands and all the intervening seas, to a point but a few miles distant from a great island continent (about the size of the present South America) which spread over the remainder of the Pacific Ocean, and included Cape Horn and parts of Patagonia.

A remarkable feature in the second map of Lemuria is the great length, and at parts the extreme narrowness, of the straits which separated the two great blocks of land into which the continent had by this time been split, and it will be observed that the straits at present existing between the islands of Bali and Lomboc coincide with a portion of the straits which then divided these two continents. It will also be seen that these straits continued in a northerly direction by the west, not by the east coast of Borneo, as conjectured by Ernst Haeckel.

With reference to the distribution of fauna and flora, and the existence of so many types common to India and Africa alike, pointed out by Mr. Blandford, it will be observed that between parts of India and great tracts of Africa there was direct land communication during the first map period, and that similar communication was partially maintained in the second map period also; while a comparison of the maps of Atlantis with those of Lemuria will demonstrate that continuous land communication existed, now at one epoch, and now at another, between so many different parts of the earth's surface, at present separated by sea, that the existing distribution of fauna and flora in the two Americas, in Europe and in Eastern lands, which has been such a puzzle to naturalists, may with perfect ease be accounted for.

The island indicated in the earlier Lemurian map as existing to the north-west of the extreme promontory of that continent, and due west of the present coast of Spain, was probably a centre from which proceeded, during long ages, the distribution of fauna and flora above referred to. For—and this is a most interesting fact—it will be seen that this island must have been the nucleus, from first to last, of the subsequent great continent of Atlantis. It existed, as we see, in these earliest Lemurian times. It was joined in the second map period to land which had previously formed part of the great Lemurian continent; and indeed, so many accretions of territory had it by this time received that it might more appropriately be called a continent than an island. It was the great mountainous region of Atlantis at its prime, when Atlantis embraced great tracts of land which have now become North and South America. It remained the mountainous region of Atlantis in its decadence, and of Ruta in the Ruta and Daitya epoch, and it practically constituted the island of Poseidonis—the last remnant of the continent of Atlantis—the final submergence of which took place in the year 9564 B.C.

A comparison of the two maps here given, along with the four maps of Atlantis, will also show that Australia and New Zealand, Madagascar, parts of Somaliland, the south of Africa, and the extreme southern portion of Patagonia are lands which have *probably* existed through all the intervening catastrophes since the early days of the Lemurian period. The same may be said of the southern parts of India and Ceylon, with the exception in the case of Ceylon, of a temporary submergence in the Ruta and Daitya epoch.

It is true there are also remains still existing of the even earlier Hyperborean continent, and they of course are the oldest known lands on the face of the earth. These are Greenland, Iceland, Spitzbergen, the most northerly parts of Norway and Sweden, and the extreme north cape of Siberia.

Japan is shown by the maps to have been above water, whether as an island, or as part of a continent, since the date of the second Lemurian map. Spain, too, has doubtless existed since that time. Spain is, therefore, with the exception of the most northerly parts of Norway and Sweden, *probably* the oldest land in Europe.

The indeterminate character of the statements just made is rendered necessary by our knowledge that there *did* occur subsidences and upheavals of different portions of the earth's surface during the ages which lay between the periods represented by the maps.

For example, soon after the date of the second Lemurian map we are informed that the whole Malay Peninsula was submerged and remained so for a long time, but a subsequent upheaval of that region must have taken place before the date of the first Atlantean map, for, what is now the Malay Peninsula is there exhibited as part of a great continent. Similarly there have been repeated minor subsidences and upheavals nearer home in more recent times, and Haeckel is perfectly correct in saying that England—he might with greater accuracy have said the islands of Great Britain and Ireland, which were then joined together—"has repeatedly been connected with the European continent, and been repeatedly separated from it."

In order to bring the subject more clearly before the mind, a tabular statement is here annexed which supplies a condensed history of the animal and plant life on our globe, bracketed—according to Haeckel—with the contemporary rock strata. Two other columns give the contemporary races of man, and such of the great cataclysms as are known to occult students.

Reptiles and Pine Forests.

From this statement it will be seen that Lemurian man lived in the age of Reptiles and Pine Forests. The amphibious monsters and the gigantic tree-ferns of the Permian age still flourished in the warm damp climates. Plesiosauri and Icthyosauri swarmed in the tepid marshes of the Mesolithic epoch, but, with the drying up of many of the inland seas, the Dinosauria—the monstrous land reptiles—gradually became the dominant type, while the Pterodactyls—the Saurians which developed bat-like wings—not only crawled on the earth, but flew through the air. The smallest of these latter were about the size of a sparrow; the largest, however, with a breadth of wing of more than sixteen feet, exceeding the largest of our living birds of to-day; while most of the Dinosauria—the Dragons—were terrible beasts of prey, colossal reptiles which attained a length of from forty to fifty feet.* Subsequent excavations have laid bare skeletons of an even larger size. Professor Ray Lankester, at a meeting of the Royal Institution on 7th January, 1904, is reported to have referred to a brontosaurus

* Ernst Haeckel's "History of Creation," Vol. ii., pp. 22-56.

Rock Strata.		Depth of Strata. Feet.	Races of Men.	Cataclysms.	Animals.	Plants.
Laurentian Cambrian Silurian	Archilithic or Primordial	70,000	First Root Race which being Astral could leave no fossil remains.		Skull-less Animals.	Forests of gigantic Tangles and other Thallus Plants.
Devonian Coal Permian	Palæolithic or Primary.	42,000	Second Root Race which was Etheric.		Fish.	Fern Forests.
Triassic Jurassic Cretaceous	Mesolithic or Secondary	15,000	Third Root Race or Lemurian.	Lemuria is said to have perished before the beginning of the Eocene age.	Reptiles.	Pine and Palm Forests.
Eocene Miocene Pliocene	Cenolithic or Tertiary.	5,000	Fourth Root Race or Atlantean.	The main Continent of Atlantis was destroyed in the Miocene period about 800,000 years ago. Second great catastrophe ? about 200,000 years ago.	Mammals.	Forests of Deciduous Trees.
Diluvial or Pleistocene Alluvial	Quarternary or Anthopolithic	500	Fifth Root Race or Aryan.	Third great catastrophe about 80,000 years ago. Final submergence of Poseidonis 9564 B.C.	More differentiated Mammals.	Cultivated Forests.

skeleton of sixty-five feet long, which had been discovered in the Oolite deposit in the southern part of the United States of America.

As it is written in the stanzas of the archaic Book of Dzyan, "Animals with bones, dragons of the deep, and flying sarpas were added to the creeping things. They that creep on the ground got wings. They of the long necks in the water became the progenitors of the fowls of the air." Modern science records her endorsement. "The class of birds as already remarked is so closely allied to Reptiles in internal structure and by embryonal development that they undoubtedly originated out of a branch of this class. . . . . The derivation of birds from reptiles first took place in the Mesolithic epoch, and this moreover probably during the Trias."*

In the vegetable kingdom this epoch also saw the pine and the palm-tree gradually displace the giant tree ferns. In the later days of the Mesolithic epoch, mammals for the first time came into existence, but the fossil remains of the mammoth and mastodon, which were their earliest representatives, are chiefly found in the subsequent strata of the Eocene and Miocene times.

The Human Kingdom.

Before making any reference to what must, even at this early date, be called the human kingdom, it must be stated that none of those who, at the present day, can lay claim to even a moderate amount of mental or spiritual culture *can* have lived in these ages. It was only with the advent of the last three sub-races of this Third Root Race that the least progressed of the first group of the Lunar Pitris began to return to incarnation, while the most advanced among them did not take birth till the early sub-races of the Atlantean period.

Indeed, Lemurian man, during at least the first half of the race, must be regarded rather as an animal destined to reach

* Ernst Haeckel's "History of Creation," Vol. ii., pp. 226-7.

humanity than as human according to our understanding of the term; for though the second and third groups of Pitris, who constituted the inhabitants of Lemuria during its first four sub-races, had achieved sufficient self-consciousness in the Lunar Manvantara to differentiate them from the animal kingdom, they had not yet received the Divine Spark which should endow them with mind and individuality—in other words, make them truly human.

Size and Consistency of Man's Body.

The evolution of this Lemurian race, therefore, constitutes one of the most obscure, as well as one of the most interesting, chapters of man's development, for during this period not only did he reach true humanity, but his body underwent the greatest physical changes, while the processes of reproduction were twice altered.

In explanation of the surprising statements which will have to be made in regard to the size and consistency of man's body at this early period it must be remembered that while the animal, vegetable and mineral kingdoms pursued the normal course, on this the fourth globe, during the Fourth Round of this Manvantara, it was ordained that humanity should run over in rapid succession the various stages through which its evolution had passed during the previous rounds of the present Manvantara. Thus the bodies of the First Root Race in which these almost mindless beings were destined to gain experience, would have appeared to us as gigantic phantoms—if indeed we could have seen them at all, for their bodies were formed of astral matter. The astral forms of the First Root Race were then gradually enveloped in a more physical casing. But though the Second Root Race may be called physical—their bodies being composed of ether—they would have been equally invisible to eyesight as it at present exists.

It was, we are told, in order that the Manu, and the Beings who aided him, might take means for improving the physical type of humanity that this epitome of the process of evolution was ordained. The highest development which the type had so far reached was the huge ape-like creature which had existed on the three physical planets, Mars, the Earth and Mercury in the Third Round. On the arrival of the human life-wave on the Earth in this the Fourth Round, a certain number, naturally, of these ape-like creatures were found in occupation—the residuum left on the planet during its period of obscuration. These, of course, joined the in-coming human stream as soon as the race became fully physical. Their bodies may not then have been absolutely discarded ; they may have been utilized for purposes of reincarnation for the most backward entities, but it was an improvement on this type which was required, and this was most easily achieved by the Manu, through working out on the astral plane in the first instance, the architype originally formed in the mind of the Logos.

From the Etheric Second Race, then, was evolved the Third —the Lemurian. Their bodies had become material, being composed of the gases, liquids and solids which constitute the three lowest sub-divisions of the physical plane, but the gases and liquids still predominated, for as yet their vertebrate structure had not solidified into bones such as ours, and they could not, therefore, stand erect. Their bones in fact were pliable as the bones of young infants now are. It was not until the middle of the Lemurian period that man developed a solid bony structure.

To explain the possibility of the process by which the etheric form evolved into a more physical form, and the soft-boned physical form ultimately developed into a structure such as man possesses to-day, it is only necessary to refer to the permanent physical atom.* Containing as it does the essence of all the forms through which

* For a further account of the permanent atoms on all the planes, and the potentialities contained in them with reference to the processes of death and re-birth, see "Man's Place in Universe." pp. 76-80.

man has passed on the physical plane, it contained consequently the potentiality of a hard-boned physical structure such as had been attained during the course of the Third Round, as well as the potentiality of an etheric form and all the phases which lie between, for it must be remembered that the physical plane consists of four grades of ether as well as the gases, liquids and solids which so many are apt to regard as alone constituting the physical. Thus, every stage of the development was a natural process, for it was a process which had been accomplished in ages long past, and all that was needed was for the Manu and the Beings who aided him, to gather round the permanent atom the appropriate kind of matter.

Organs of Vision.

The organs of vision of these creatures before they developed bones were of a rudimentary nature, at least such was the condition of the two eyes in front with which they sought for their food upon the ground. But there was a third eye at the back of the head, the atrophied remnant of which of which is now known as the *pineal gland*. This, as we know, is *now* a centre solely of astral vision, but at the epoch of which we are speaking it was the chief centre not only of astral but of physical sight. Referring to reptiles which had become extinct, Professor Ray Lankester, in a recent lecture at the Royal Institution, is reported to have drawn special attention "to the size of the parietal foramen in the skull which showed that in the ichthyosaurs the parietal or pineal eye on the top of the head must have been very large." In this respect he went on to say mankind were inferior to these big sea lizards, "for we had lost the third eye which might be studied in the common lizard, or better in the great blue lizard of the South of France."*

Somewhat before the middle of the Lemurian period, probably during the evolution of the third sub-race, the gigantic gelatinous

* The "Standard," 8th Jan., 1904.

body began slowly to solidify and the soft-boned limbs developed into a bony structure. These primitive creatures were now able to stand upright, and the two eyes in the face gradually became the chief organs of physical sight, though the third eye still remained to some extent an organ of physical sight also, and this it did till the very end of the Lemurian epoch. It, of course, remained an actual organ, as it still is a potential focus, of psychic vision. This psychic vision continued to be an attribute of the race not only throughout the whole Lemurian period, but well into the days of Atlantis.

A curious fact to note is that when the race first attained the power of standing and moving in an upright position, they could walk backwards with almost as great ease as forwards. This may be accounted for not only by the capacity for vision possessed by the third eye, but doubtless also by the curious projection at the heels which will presently be referred to.

Description of Lemurian Man.

The following is a description of a man who belonged to one of the later sub-races—probably the fifth. "His stature was gigantic, somewhere between twelve and fifteen feet. His skin was very dark, being of a yellowish brown colour. He had a long lower jaw, a strangely flattened face, eyes small but piercing and set curiously far apart, so that he could see sideways as well as in front, while the eye at the back of the head—on which part of the head no hair, of course, grew—enabled him to see in that direction also. He had no forehead, but there seemed to be a roll of flesh where it should have been. The head sloped backwards and upwards in a rather curious way. The arms and legs (especially the former) were longer in proportion than ours, and could not be perfectly straightened either at elbows or knees; the hands and feet were enormous, and the heels projected backwards in an ungainly way. The figure was draped in a loose robe of skin, something like rhinoceros hide, but more scaly, probably the skin of some animal of which we now know only through its fossil remains. Round his head, on which the hair was quite short, was twisted another piece of skin to which were attached tassels of bright red, blue and other colours. In his left hand he held a sharpened staff, which was doubtless used for defence or attack. It was about the height of his own body, *viz.*, twelve to fifteen feet. In his right hand was twisted the end of a long rope made of some sort of creeping plant, by which he led a huge and hideous reptile, somewhat resembling the Plesiosaurus. The Lemurians actually domesticated these creatures, and trained them to employ their strength in hunting other animals. The appearance of the man gave an unpleasant sensation, but he was not entirely uncivilised, being an average common-place specimen of his day."

Many were even less human in appearance than the individual here described, but the seventh sub-race developed a superior type, though very unlike any living men of the present time. While retaining the projecting lower jaw, the thick heavy lips, the flattened face, and the uncanny looking eyes, they had by this time developed something which might be called a forehead, while the curious projection of the heel had been considerably reduced. In one branch of this seventh sub-race, the head might be described as almost egg-shaped—the small end of the egg being uppermost, with the eyes wide apart and very near the top. The stature had perceptibly decreased, and the appearance of the hands, feet and limbs generally had become more like those of the negroes of to-day. These people developed an important and long-lasting civilisation, and for thousands of years dominated most of the other tribes who dwelt on the vast Lemurian continent, and even at the end, when racial decay seemed to be overtaking them, they secured another long lease of life and power by inter-marriage with the Rmoahals—the first sub-race of the

Atlanteans. The progeny, while retaining many Third Race characteristics, of course, really belonged to the Fourth Race, and thus naturally acquired fresh power of development. Their general appearance now became not unlike that of some American Indians, except that their skin had a curious bluish tinge not now to be seen.

But surprising as were the changes in the size, consistency, and appearance of man's body during this period, the alterations in the process of reproduction are still more astounding. A reference to the systems which now obtain among the lower kingdoms of nature may help us in the consideration of the subject.

Processes of Reproduction.

After instancing the simplest processes of propagation by self-division, and by the formation of buds (Gemmatio), Haeckel proceeds, "A third mode of non-sexual propagation, that of the formation of germ-buds (Polysporogonia) is intimately connected with the formation of buds. In the case of the lower, imperfect organisms, among animals, especially in the case of the plant-like animals and worms, we very frequently find that in the interior of an individual composed of many cells, a small group of cells separates itself from those surrounding it, and that this small isolated group gradually develops itself into an individual, which becomes like the parent and sooner or later comes out of it. . . . . . . The formation of germ buds is evidently but little different from real budding. But, on the other hand, it is connected with a fourth kind of non-sexual propagation, which almost forms a transition to sexual reproduction, namely, the formation of germ cells (Monosporogonia). In this case it is no longer a group of cells but a single cell, which separates itself from the surrounding cells in the interior of the producing organism, and which becomes further developed after it has come out of its parent. . . . . .

Sexual or amphigonic propagation (Amphigonia) is the usual method of propagation among all higher animals and plants. It is evident that it has only developed at a very late period of the earth's history, from non-sexual propagation, and apparently in the first instance from the method of propagation by germ-cells. . . . . . In all the chief forms of non-sexual propagation mentioned above—in fission, in the formation of buds, germ-buds, and germ-cells—the separated cell or group of cells was able by itself to develop into a new individual, but in the case of sexual propagation, the cell must first be fructified by another generative substance. The fructifying sperm must first mix with the germ-cell (the egg) before the latter can develop into a new individual. These two generative substances, the sperm and the egg, are either produced by one and the same individual hermaphrodite (Hermaphroditismus) or by two different individuals (sexual-separation).

" The simpler and more ancient form of sexual propagation is through double-sexed individuals. It occurs in the great majority of plants, but only in a minority of animals, for example, in the garden snails, leeches, earth-worms, and many other worms. Every single individual among hermaphrodites produces within itself materials of both sexes—eggs and sperm. In most of the higher plants every blossom contains both the male organ (stamens and anther) and the female organ (style and germ). Every garden snail produces in one part of its sexual gland eggs, and in another part sperm. Many hermaphrodites can fructify themselves ; in others, however, reciprocal fructification of both hermaphrodites is necessary for causing the development of the eggs. This latter case is evidently a transition to sexual separation.

" Sexual separation, which characterises the more complicated of the two kinds of sexual reproduction, has evidently been developed from the condition of hermaphroditism at a late period of the organic history of the world. It is at present the universal method of propagation of the higher animals. . . . . . The so-called virginal reproduction (Parthenogenesis) offers an interesting form of transition from sexual reproduction to the non-sexual formation of germ-cells which most resembles it. . . . In this case germ-cells which otherwise appear and are formed exactly like egg-cells, become capable of developing themselves into new individuals without requiring the fructifying seed. The most remarkable and the most instructive of the different parthenogenetic phenomena are furnished by those cases in which the same germ-cells, according as they are fructified or not, produce different kinds of individuals. Among our common honey bees, a male individual (a drone) arises out of the eggs of the queen, if the egg has not been fructified; a female (a queen, or working bee) if the egg has been fructified. It is evident from this, that in reality there exists no wide chasm between sexual and non-sexual reproduction, but that both modes of reproduction are directly connected."*

Now, the interesting fact in connection with the evolution of Third Race man on Lemuria, is that his mode of reproduction ran through phases which were closely analogous with some of the processes above described. Sweat-born, egg-born and Androgyne are the terms used in the Secret Doctrine.

"Almost sexless, in its early beginnings, it became bisexual or androgynous; very gradually, of course. The passage from the former to the latter transformation required numberless generations, during which the simple cell that issued from the earliest parent (the two in one), first developed into a bisexual being; and then the cell, becoming a regular egg, gave forth a unisexual creature. The Third Race mankind is the most mys-

* Ernst Haeckel's "The History of Creation," 2nd ed., Vol. i., pp. 193-8.

terious of all the hitherto developed five Races. The mystery of the "How" of the generation of the distinct sexes must, of course, be very obscure here, as it is the business of an embryologist and a specialist, the present work giving only faint outlines of the process. But it is evident that the units of the Third Race humanity began to separate in their pre-natal shells, or eggs, and to issue out of them as distinct male and female babes, ages after the appearance of its early progenitors. And, as time rolled on its geological periods, the newly born sub-races began to lose their natal capacities. Toward the end of the fourth *sub-race*, the babe lost its faculty of walking as soon as liberated from its shell, and by the end of the fifth, mankind was born under the same conditions and by the same identical process as our historical generations. This required, of course, millions of years."*

Lemurian Races still Inhabiting the Earth.

It may be as well again to repeat that the almost mindless creatures who inhabited such bodies as have been above described during the early sub-races of the Lemurian period can scarcely be regarded as completely human. It was only after the separation of the sexes, when their bodies had become densely physical, that they became human even in appearance. It must be remembered that the beings we are speaking of, though embracing the second and third groups of the Lunar Pitris, must also have been largely recruited from the animal kingdom of that (the Lunar) Manvantara. The degraded remnants of the Third Root Race who still inhabit the earth may be recognised in the aborigines of Australia, the Andaman Islanders, some hill tribes of India, the Tierra-del-Fuegans, the Bushmen of Africa, and some other savage tribes. The entities now inhabiting these bodies must have belonged to the animal kingdom in the early part of *this* Manvantara. It was probably during the evolution of the Lemurian race and

*"The Secret Doctrine," Vol. ii., p. 197.

before the " door was shut " on the entities thronging up from below, that these attained the human kingdom.

The shameful acts of the mindless men at the first separation of the sexes had best be referred to in the words of the stanzas of the archaic Book of Dzyan. No commentary is needed. **Sin of the Mindless.**

" During the Third Race the boneless animals grew and changed, they became animals with bones, their chayas became solid.

" The animals separated first. They began to breed. The two-fold man separated also. He said, ' Let us as they ; let us unite and make creatures.' They did.

" And those that had no spark took huge she-animals unto them. They begat upon them dumb races. Dumb they were themselves. But their tongues untied. The tongues of their progeny remained still. Monsters they bred. A race of crooked red-hair-covered monsters going on all fours. A dumb race to keep the shame untold." (And an ancient commentary adds ' when the Third separated and fell into sin by breeding men-animals, these (the animals) became ferocious, and men and they mutually destructive. Till then, there was no sin, no life taken.').

" Seeing which the Lhas who had not built men, wept, saying. ' The Amanasa [mindless] have defiled our future abodes. This is Karma. Let us dwell in the others. Let us teach them better lest worse should happen.' They did.

" Then all men became endowed with Manas. They saw the sin of the mindless."

The anatomical resemblance between Man and the higher Ape, so frequently cited by Darwinists as pointing to some ancestor common to both, presents an interesting problem, the proper solution of which is to be sought for in the esoteric explanation of the genesis of the pithecoid stocks. **Origin of the Pithecoid and the Anthropoid Apes.**

Now, we gather from the Secret Doctrine* that the descendants of these semi-human monsters described above as originating in the sin of the "mindless," having through long centuries dwindled in size and become more densely physical, culminated in a race of Apes at the time of the Miocene period, from which in their turn are descended the pithecoids of to-day. With these Apes of the Miocene period, however, the Atlanteans of that age renewed the sin of the "mindless"—this time with full responsibility, and the resultants of their crime are the species of Apes now known as Anthropoid.

We are given to understand that in the coming Sixth Root Race, these anthropoids will obtain human incarnation, in the bodies doubtless of the lowest races then existing upon earth.

That part of the Lemurian continent where the separation of the sexes took place, and where both the fourth and the fifth sub-races flourished, is to be found in the earlier of the two maps. It lay to the east of the mountainous region of which the present Island of Madagascar formed a part, and thus occupied a central position around the smaller of the two great lakes.

Origin of Language.

As stated in the stanzas of Dzyan above quoted, the men of that epoch, even though they had become completely physical, still remained speechless. Naturally the astral and etherial ancestors of this Third Root Race had no need to produce a series of sounds in order to convey their thoughts, living as they did in astral and etherial conditions, but when man became physical he could not for long remain dumb. We are told that the sounds which these primitive men made to express their thoughts were at first composed entirely of vowels. In the slow course of evolution the consonant sounds gradually came into use, but the development of language from first to last on the continent of Lemuria never reached beyond the mono-

* Vol. ii., pp. 683 and 689.

syllabic phase. The Chinese language of to-day is the sole great lineal descendant of ancient Lemurian speech* for "the whole human race was at that time of one language and of one lip."†

In Humboldt's classification of language, the Chinese, as we know, is called the *isolating* as distinguished from the more highly evolved *agglutinative*, and the still more highly evolved *inflectional*. Readers of the *Story of Atlantis* may remember that many different languages were developed on that continent, but all belonged to the *agglutinative*, or, as Max Müller prefers to call it, the *combinatory* type, while the still higher development of *inflectional* speech, in the Aryan and Semitic tongues, was reserved for our own era of the Fifth Root Race.

The First Taking of Life.

The first instance of sin, the first taking of life—quoted above from an old commentary on the stanzas of Dzyan, may be taken as indicative of the attitude which was then inaugurated between the human and the animal kingdom, and which has since attained such awful proportions, not only between men and animals, but between the different races of men themselves. And this opens up a most interesting avenue of thought.

The fact that Kings and Emperors consider it necessary or appropriate, on all state occasions, to appear in the garb of one of the fighting branches of their service, is a significant indication of the apotheosis reached by the combative qualities in man! The custom doubtless comes down from a time when the King was the warrior-chief, and when his kingship was acknowledged solely in virtue of his being the chief warrior. But now that the Fifth Root Race is in ascendency, whose chief characteristic and function is the development of intellect, it might have been expected that the dominant attribute of the Fourth Root Race

* It must, however, be noted that the Chinese *people* are mainly descended from the fourth or Turanian sub-race of the Fourth Root Race.

† "Secret Doctrine," Vol. ii., p. 198.

would have been a little less conspicuously paraded. But the era of one race overlaps another, and though, as we know, the leading races of the world all belong to the Fifth Root Race, the vast majority of its inhabitants still belong to the Fourth, and it would appear that the Fifth Root Race has not yet outstripped Fourth Race characteristics, for it is by infinitely slow degrees that man's evolution is accomplished.

It will be interesting here to summarise the history of this strife and bloodshed from its genesis during these far-off ages on Lemuria.

From the information placed before the writer it would seem that the antagonism between men and animals was developed first. With the evolution of man's physical body, suitable food for that body naturally became an urgent need, so that in addition to the antagonism brought about by the necessity of self-defence against the now ferocious animals, the desire of food also urged men to their slaughter, and as we have seen above, one of the first uses they made of their budding mentality was to train animals to act as hunters in the chase.

The element of strife having once been kindled, men soon began to use weapons of offence against each other. The causes of aggression were naturally the same as those which exist to-day among savage communities. The possession of any desirable object by one of his fellows was sufficient inducement for a man to attempt to take it by force. Nor was strife limited to single acts of aggression. As among savages to-day, bands of marauders would attack and pillage the communities who dwelt at a distance from their own village. But to this extent only, we are told, was warfare organised on Lemuria, even down to the end of its seventh sub-race.

It was reserved for the Atlanteans to develop the principle of strife on organised lines—to collect and to drill armies and to build navies. This principle of strife was indeed the fundamental characteristic of the Fourth Root Race. All through the Atlantean period, as we know, warfare was the order of the day, and battles were constantly fought on land and sea. And so deeply rooted in man's nature during the Atlantean period did this principle of strife become, that even now the most intellectually developed of the Aryan races are ready to war upon each other.

The Arts.

To trace the development of the Arts among the Lemurians, we must start with the history of the fifth sub-race. The separation of the sexes was now fully accomplished, and man inhabited a completely physical body, though it was still of gigantic stature. The offensive and defensive war with the monstrous beasts of prey had already begun, and men had taken to living in huts. To build their huts they tore down trees, and piled them up in a rude fashion. At first each separate family lived in its own clearing in the jungle, but they soon found it safer, as a defence against the wild beasts, to draw together and live in small communities. Their huts, too, which had been formed of rude trunks of trees, they now learnt to build with boulders of stone, while the weapons with which they attacked, or defended themselves against the Dinosauria and other wild beasts, were spears of sharpened wood, similar to the staff held by the man whose appearance is described above.

Up to this time agriculture was unknown, and the uses of fire had not been discovered. The food of their boneless ancestors who crawled on the earth were such things as they could find on the surface of the ground or just below it. Now that they walked erect many of the wild forest trees provided them with nuts and berries, but their chief article of food was the flesh of the beasts and reptiles which they slew, tore in pieces, and devoured.

Teachers of the Lemurian Race.

But now there occurred an event pregnant with consequences the most momentous in the history of the human race. An event too full of mystical import, for its narration brings into view Beings who belonged to entirely different systems of evolution, and who nevertheless came at this epoch to be associated with our humanity.

The lament of the Lhas " who had not built men " at seeing their future abodes defiled, is at first sight far from intelligible. Though the descent of these Beings into human bodies is not the chief event to which we have to refer, some explanation of its cause and its result must first be attempted. Now, we are given to understand that these Lhas were the highly evolved humanity of some system of evolution which had run its course at a period in the infinitely far-off past. They had reached a high stage of development on their chain of worlds, and since its dissolution had passed the intervening ages in the bliss of some Nirvanic condition. But their karma now necessitated a return to some field of action and of physical causes, and as they had not yet fully learnt the lesson of compassion, their temporary task now lay in becoming guides and teachers of the Lemurian race, who then required all the help and guidance they could get.

But other Beings also took up the task—in this case voluntarily. These came from the scheme of evolution which has Venus as its one physical planet. That scheme has already reached the Seventh Round of its planets in its Fifth Manvantara; its humanity therefore stands at a far higher level than ordinary mankind on this earth has yet attained. They are " divine " while we are only " human." The Lemurians, as we have seen, were then merely on the verge of attaining true manhood. It was to supply a temporary need—the education of our infant humanity—that these divine Beings came—as we possibly, long ages hence, may similarly be called to give a helping hand to the beings struggling up to manhood on the Jupiter or the Saturn chain. Under their guidance and influence the Lemurians rapidly advanced in mental growth. The stirring of their minds with feelings of love and reverence for those whom they felt to be infinitely wiser and greater than themselves naturally resulted in efforts of imitation, and so the necessary advance in mental growth was achieved which transformed the higher mental sheath into a vehicle capable of carrying over the human characteristics from life to life, thus warranting that outpouring of the Divine Life which endowed the recipient with individual immortality. As expressed in the archaic stanzas of Dzyan, "Then all men became endowed with Manas."

A great distinction, however, must be noted between the coming of the exalted Beings from the Venus scheme and that of those described as the highly evolved humanity of some previous system of evolution. The former, as we have seen, were under no karmic impulse. They came as men to live and work among them, but they were not required to assume their physical limitations, being in a position to provide appropriate vehicles for themselves.

The Lhas on the other hand had actually to be born in the bodies of the race as it then existed. Better would it have been both for them and for the race if there had been no hesitation or delay on their part in taking up their Karmic task, for the sin of the mindless and all its consequences would have been avoided. Their task, too, would have been an easier one, for it consisted not only in acting as guides and teachers, but in improving the racial type—in short, in evolving out of the half-human, half-animal form then existing, the physical body of the man to be.

It must be remembered that up to this time the Lemurian race consisted of the second and third groups of the Lunar Pitris. But now that they were approaching the level reached on the

Lunar chain by the first group of Pitris, it became necessary for these again to return to incarnation, and this they did all through the fifth, sixth and seventh sub-races (indeed, some did not take birth till the Atlantean period), so that the impetus given to the progress of the race was a cumulative force.

The positions occupied by the divine beings from the Venus chain were naturally those of rulers, instructors in religion, and teachers of the arts, and it is in this latter capacity that a reference to the arts taught by them comes to our aid in the consideration of the history of this early race.

The Arts continued.

Under the guidance of their divine teachers the people began to learn the use of fire, and the means by which it could be obtained, at first by friction, and later on by the use of flints and iron. They were taught to explore for metals, to smelt and to mould them, and instead of spears of sharpened wood they now began to use spears tipped with sharpened metal.

They were also taught to dig and till the ground and to cultivate the seeds of wild grain till it improved in type. This cultivation carried on through the vast ages which have since elapsed has resulted in the evolution of the various cereals which we now possess—barley, oats, maize, millet, etc. But an exception must here be noted. Wheat was not evolved upon this planet like the other cereals. It was a gift of the divine beings who brought it from Venus ready for the food of man. Nor was wheat their only gift. The one animal form whose type has not been evolved on our chain of worlds is that of the bee. It, too, was brought from Venus.

The Lemurians now also began to learn the art of spinning and weaving fabrics with which to clothe themselves. These were made of the coarse hair of a species of animal now extinct, but which bore some resemblance to the llamas of to-day, the ancestors of which they may possibly have been. We have seen above that the earliest articles of clothing of Lemurian man were robes of skin stripped from the beasts he had slain. These skins he still continued to wear on the colder parts of the continent, but he now learnt to cure and dress the skin in some rude fashion.

One of the first things the people were taught was the use of fire in the preparation of their food, and whether it was the flesh of animals they slew or the pounded grains of wheat, their modes of cooking were closely analogous to those we hear of as existing to-day among savage communities. With reference to the gift of wheat so marvellously brought from Venus, the divine rulers doubtless realised the advisability of at once procuring such food for the people, for they must have known that it would take many generations before the cultivation of the wild seeds could provide an adequate supply.

Rude and barbarous as were the people during the period of the fifth and sixth sub-races, such of them as had the privilege of coming in contact with their divine teachers were naturally inspired with such feelings of reverence and worship as helped to lift them out of their savage condition. The constant influx, too, of more intelligent beings from the first group of the Lunar Pitris, who were then beginning to return to incarnation, helped the attainment of a more civilised state.

Great Cities and Statues.

During the later part of the sixth, and the seventh subrace they learnt to build great cities. These appear to have been of cyclopean architecture, corresponding with the gigantic bodies of the race. The first cities were built on that extended mountainous region of the continent which included, as will be seen in the first map, the present Island of Madagascar. Another great city is described in the "Secret Doctrine"* as having been entirely built of blocks of lava. It lay some 30 miles west of the present Easter Island, and

* Vol. ii., p. 317.

it was subsequently destroyed by a series of volcanic eruptions. The gigantic statues of Easter Island—measuring as most of them do about 27 feet in height by 8 feet across the shoulders—were probably intended to be representative not only of the features, but of the height of those who carved them, or it may be of their ancestors, for it was probably in the later ages of the Lemuro-Atlanteans that the statues were erected. It will be observed that by the second map period, the continent of which Easter Island formed a part had been broken up and Easter Island itself had become a comparatively small island, though of considerably greater dimensions than it retains to-day.

Civilisations of comparative importance arose on different parts of the continent and the great islands where the inhabitants built cities and dwelt in settled communities, but large tribes who were also partially civilised continued to lead a nomadic and patriarchial life; while other parts of the land—in many cases the least accessible, as in our own times—were peopled by tribes of extremely low type.

Religion. With so primitive a race of men, at the best, there was but little in the shape of religion that they could be taught. Simple rules of conduct and the most elementary precepts of morality were all that they were fitted to understand or to practise. During the evolution of the seventh sub-race, it is true that their divine instructors taught them some primitive form of worship and imparted the knowledge of a Supreme Being whose symbol was represented as the Sun.

Destruction of the Continent. Unlike the subsequent fate of Atlantis, which was submerged by great tidal waves, the continent of Lemuria perished by volcanic action. It was raked by the burning ashes and the red-hot dust from numberless volcanoes. Earthquakes and volcanic eruptions, it is true, heralded each of the great catastrophes which overtook Atlantis, but when the land had been shaken and rent, the sea rushed in and completed the work, and most of the inhabitants perished by drowning. The Lemurians, on the other hand, met their doom chiefly by fire or suffocation. Another marked contrast between the fate of Lemuria and Atlantis was that while four great catastrophes completed the destruction of the latter, the former was slowly eaten away by internal fires, for, from the time when the disintegrating process began towards the end of the first map period, there was no cessation from the fiery activity, and whether in one part of the continent or another, the volcanic action was incessant, while the invariable sequence was the subsidence and total disappearance of the land, just as in the case of Krakatoa in 1883.

So closely analogous was the eruption of Mount Pelée, which caused the destruction of St. Pièrre, the capital of Martinique, about two years ago, to the whole series of volcanic catastrophes on the continent of Lemuria, that the description of the former given by some of the survivors may be of interest. " An immense black cloud had suddenly burst forth from the crater of Mont Pelée and rushed with terrific velocity upon the city, destroying everything—inhabitants, houses and vegetation alike—that it found in its path. In two or three minutes it passed over, and the city was a blazing pyre of ruins. In both islands [Martinique and St. Vincent] the eruptions were characterised by the sudden discharge of immense quantities of red-hot dust, mixed with steam, which flowed down the steep hillsides with an ever-increasing velocity. In St. Vincent this had filled many valleys to a depth of between 100 feet and 200 feet, and months after the eruptions was still very hot, and the heavy rains which then fell thereon caused enormous explosions, producing clouds of steam and dust that shot upwards to a height of from 1500 feet to 2000 feet, and filled the rivers with black boiling mud." Captain

Freeman, of the "Roddam," then described "à thrilling experience which he and his party had at Martinique. One night, when they were lying at anchor in a little sloop about a mile from St. Pièrre, the mountain exploded in a way that was apparently an exact repetition of the original eruption. It was not entirely without warning; hence they were enabled to sail at once a mile or two further away, and thus probably saved their lives. In the darkness they saw the summit glow with a bright red light; then soon, with loud detonations, great red-hot stones were projected into the air and rolled down the slopes. A few minutes later a prolonged rumbling noise was heard, and in an instant was followed by a red-hot avalanche of dust, which rushed out of the crater and rolled down the side with a terrific speed, which they estimated at about 100 miles an hour, with a temperature of 1000° centigrade. As to the probable explanation of these phenomena, no lava, he said, had been seen to flow from either of the volcanoes, but only steam and fine hot dust. The volcanoes were, therefore, of the explosive type; and from all his observations he had concluded that the absence of lava-flows was due to the material within the crater being partly solid, or at least highly viscous, so that it could not flow like an ordinary lava-stream. Since his return this theory had received striking confirmation, for it was now known that within the crater of Mont Pelée there was no lake of molten lava, but that a solid pillar of red-hot rock was slowly rising upwards in a great conical, sharp-pointed hill, until it might finally overtop the old summit of the mountain. It was nearly 1000 feet high, and slowly grew as it was forced upwards by pressure from beneath, while every now and then explosions of steam took place, dislodging large pieces from its summit or its sides. Steam was set free within this mass as it cooled, and the rock then passed into a dangerous and highly explosive condition, such that an explosion must sooner or later take place, which shivered a great part of the mass into fine red-hot dust."*

A reference to the first Lemurian map will show that in the lake lying to the south-east of the extensive mountainous region there was an island which consisted of little more than one great mountain. This mountain was a very active volcano. The four mountains which lay to the south-west of the lake were also active volcanoes, and in this region it was that the disruption of the continent began. The seismic cataclysms which followed the volcanic eruptions caused such wide-spread damage that by the second map period a large portion of the southern part of the continent had been submerged.

A marked characteristic of the land surface in early Lemurian times was the great number of lakes and marshes, as well as the innumerable volcanoes. Of course, all these are not shown on the map. Only some of the great mountains which were volcanoes, and only some of the largest lakes are there indicated.

Another volcano on the north-east coast of the continent began its destructive work at an early date. Earthquakes completed the disruption, and it seems probable that the sea shown in the second map as dotted with small islands to the south-east of the present Japan, indicates the area of seismic disturbance.

In the first map it will be seen that there were lakes in the centre of what is now the island-continent of Australia—lakes where the land is at present exceedingly dry and parched. By the second map period those lakes had disappeared, and it seems natural to conjecture that the districts where those lakes lay, must, during the eruptions of the great volcanoes which lay to the south-east (between the present Australia and New Zealand), have been so raked with red-hot volcanic dust that the very water-springs were dried up.

* The "Times," 14th Sept., 1903.

Founding of the Atlantean Race.

In concluding this sketch, a reference to the process by which the Fourth Root Race was brought into existence, will appropriately bring to an end what we know of the story of Lemuria and link it on to that of Atlantis.

It may be remembered from previous writings on the subject that it was from the *fifth* or Semitic sub-race of the Fourth Root Race that was chosen the nucleus destined to become our great Fifth or Aryan Root Race. It was not, however, until the time of the *seventh* sub-race on Lemuria that humanity was sufficiently developed physiologically to warrant the choice of individuals fit to become the parents of a new Root Race. So it was from the seventh sub-race that the segregation was effected. The colony was first settled on land which occupied the site of the present Ashantee and Western Nigeria. A reference to the second map will show this as a promontory lying to the north-west of the island-continent which embraced the Cape of Good Hope and parts of western Africa. Having been guarded for generations from any admixture with a lower type, the colony gradually increased in numbers, and the time came when it was ready to receive and to hand on the new impulse to physical heredity which the Manu was destined to impart.

Students of Theosophy are aware that, up to the present day, no one belonging to our humanity has been in a position to undertake the exalted office of Manu, though it is stated that the founding of the coming Sixth Root Race will be entrusted to the guidance of one of our Masters of Wisdom—one who, while belonging to our humanity, has nevertheless reached a most exalted level in the Divine Hierarchy.

In the case we are considering—the founding of the Fourth Root Race—it was one of the Adepts from Venus who undertook the duties of the Manu. Naturally he belonged to a very high order, for it must be understood that the Beings who came from the Venus system as rulers and teachers of our infant humanity did *not* all stand at the same level. It is this circumstance which furnishes a reason for the remarkable fact that may, in conclusion, be stated—namely, that there existed in Lemuria a Lodge of Initiation.

A Lodge of Initiation.

Naturally it was not for the benefit of the Lemurian race that the Lodge was founded. Such of them as were sufficiently advanced were, it is true, taught by the Adept Gurus, but the instruction they required was limited to the explanation of a few physical phenomena, such as the fact that the earth moves round the sun, or to the explanation of the different appearance which physical objects assumed for them when subjected alternately to their physical sight and their astral vision.

It was, of course, for the sake of those who, while endowed with the stupendous powers of transferring their consciousness from the planet Venus to this our earth, and of providing for their use and their work while here appropriate vehicles in which to function, were yet pursuing the course of their own evolution.* For their sake it was—for the sake of those who, having entered the Path, had only reached the lower grades, that this Lodge of Initiation was founded.

Though, as we know, the goal of normal evolution is greater and more glorious than can, from our present standpoint, be well imagined, it is by no means synonymous with that expansion of consciousness which, combined with and alone made possible by, the purification and ennoblement of character, constitute the heights to which the Pathway of Initiation leads.

* The heights reached by them will find their parallel when our humanity will, countless aeons hence, have reached the Sixth Round of our chain of worlds, and the same transcendent powers will be the possession of ordinary mankind in those far-off ages.

The investigation into what constitutes this purification and ennoblement of character, and the endeavour to realise what that expansion of consciousness really means are subjects which have been written of elsewhere.

Suffice it now to point out that the founding of a Lodge of Initiation for the sake of Beings who came from another scheme of evolution is an indication of the unity of object and of aim in the government and the guidance of *all* the schemes of evolution brought into existence by our Solar Logos. Apart from the normal course in our own scheme, there is, we know, a Path by which He may be directly reached, which every son of man in his progress through the ages is privileged to hear of, and to tread, if he so chooses. We find that this was so in the Venus scheme also, and we may presume it is or will be so in all the schemes which form part of our Solar system. This Path is the Path of Initiation, and the end to which leads is the same for all, and that end is Union with God.